UP
CLOSE

SEA LIFE

A CLOSE-UP PHOTOGRAPHIC LOOK INSIDE YOUR WORLD

Quarto is the authority on a wide range of topics.
Quarto educates, entertains and enriches the lives of our readers—
enthusiasts and lovers of hands-on living.
www.quartoknows.com

Project Editor: Heidi Fiedler
Written by Heidi Fiedler

Cover photography by Audrey Narchuk.
Photograph on pages 34–35 by Linden Gledhill. Photographs on pages 16, 18, 36, 42, and 54 by Henry Jager.
Photographs on pages 24 and 44 by Audrey Narchuk. Photographs on pages 7 (center image),
22, 26–28, 38, 40, 50, 52, and 60 by Alexander Semenov.
Photograph on page 8 by Todd Winner.
All other images © Shutterstock.

6 Orchard Road, Suite 100
Lake Forest, CA 92630
quartoknows.com
Visit our blogs @quartoknows.com

Printed in China
1 3 5 7 9 10 8 6 4 2

Are You Ready for Your Close-up?

Can you feel your brain tickling? That's the magic of looking at something way UP CLOSE. It transforms the ordinary into something new and strange and inspires everyone from hi-tech shutterbugs and supersmart scientists to look again. So let's turn the ZOOM up to eleven and discover a whole new way of seeing the world.

How Eye See the World

"Whatcha lookin' at?" That's the question people have been asking each other for thousands of years. The first humans observed interesting—and important—things like woolly mammoths, lightning, and each other. Early artists moved on to painting and drawing what they saw. Finally, in 1862, photography allowed people to capture what they saw in new and amazing ways.

Today, photographs are everywhere. Cereal boxes, bulletin boards, and T-shirts are all home to photos. A simple image search online can produce adorable images of bright-eyed babies or stark, white, snowy landscapes. Photographers capture everything from moments of joy and pain to the wonders that exist in the cracks and hidden layers of our busy world. They focus their attention on a huge range of subjects, and the images they produce reveal how everyone sees the world in their own unique way.

The History of Photography

Black & White Photography

1839
Daguerreotypes capture rough images.

1859
Photography goes panoramic.

1862
Nicéphore Niépce creates the first photograph. It takes 8 hours.

1877
Eadweard Muybridge invents a way to shoot objects—like horses—in motion.

Color
Photography

1888
Kodak™ produces the first mass-produced camera.

1912
The 35mm camera takes center stage.

1930
Flash bulbs help photographers capture images in low light.

1939
An electron microscope reveals what a virus looks like.

1935
New techniques make color photography shine.

1946
Zoomar produces the zoom lens.

Digital
Photography

1976
Canon® produces the first camera with a microprocessor.

"**Photography**...has **little** to do with the things you **see** and **everything** to do with the **way** you **see** them."
—Elliott Erwitt

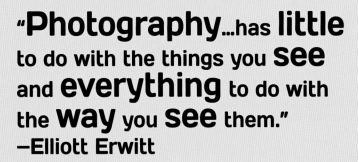

1992
The first JPEG is produced.

2015
Instagram is home to over 20 billion images.

Extreme Close-up!

Photography has been helping people express how they see the world for nearly 200 years, and in that time, things have gone way beyond taking a simple shot of a horse or a sunset. Today, photographers are pushing the limits of technology.

Macro photographers use large lenses to get WAY up close to their subjects. They can magnify an object to more than five times its size, using special lenses that reveal patterns and textures that wow viewers.

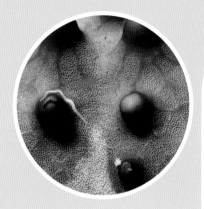

Micro photography goes even further. It uses a microscope to reveal details humans could never see before. It can make a beetle look like a glowing planet or a priceless piece of jewelry.

The deep blue oceans of our planet are some of the last places on Earth that have yet to be explored. And photographers are leading the way. Some are scientists, studying creatures that have no names. Others simply love being underwater, where life is more colorful and stranger than we could ever imagine. Take a look!

Getting the Shot

Photographers choose where and how they want to work based on what type of images they want to produce.

Out in the Field

Macro photographers can take their giant lenses underwater to capture sea life in its natural environment.

In the Studio

Working inside lets photographers have more control over the lighting, the angle of the camera, and their subject.

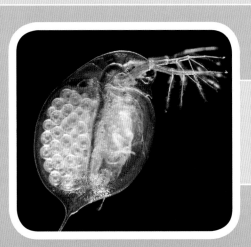

Under the Microscope

A microscope allows photographers to look at their subjects in even more detail.

The Abyss

Down,
Down,
Down,
It goes.
Where it stops,
No one knows.
Lost in an underwater maze.
There's no map. Just haze.

Bird's Eye View

But up, up, up…and the abyss is transformed.
With a hard, beak-like mouth and colorful scales,
the parrotfish is easy to recognize.
Welcome to the jungle.

Pajama Party

At night, parrotfish produce a layer of mucus around their heads. But this isn't just a soft pillow to rest on. Experts think the mucus masks the fish's smell, which makes it less likely to be eaten while it sleeps.

Scientific Name:
  Scaridae
Size: 1 to 4 feet long
Habitat: Coral reefs
  around the world
Diet: Algae and coral

Some have called the **parrotfish** the most **colorful** fish in the world.

An Unforgettable Handshake

Long alien fingers beckon you closer. But these hands don't belong to little green men. This is a coral—a creature made up of many tiny animals that have grown a hard skeleton. These creatures are so strange; they're almost like aliens living among us. (But they've lived underwater for more than 50 million years!)

Scientific Name: Acroporidae
Size: Branches can grow up to 7 feet
Habitat: Warm ocean water up to 100 feet deep
Diet: Algae living inside the coral produce food for the coral

These **coral** are known as **staghorn** or **elkhorn** because their **branches** sometimes look like **antlers**.

The Stories They Could Tell

The largest coral reefs are also the oldest. Acropora corals can grow about 4 inches per year.

A Big (Beautiful) Blob

The great explorers of the world travel by foot, on trains, and up above our heads in planes. But jellyfish float. And their movements are mesmerizing. Jellyfish come in all shapes and sizes, and their names are just as strange. There's egg-yolk jellyfish, blubber jelly, hair, moon, mosaic, and more.

Scientific Name:
There are more than 200 types of jellies
Size: Can range between 1 and 75 inches
Habitat: Around the world
Diet: Tiny crustaceans, small fish, plankton, and other jellyfish

Many lion's **mane** jellies are **bioluminescent** and act as their own **flashlight** in the deep **dark** waters of the **sea**.

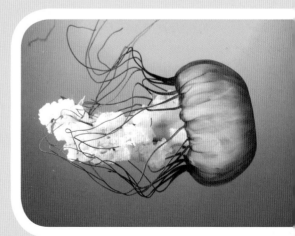

Tangled Tentacles

If you think it's hard to untangle the wires on your earphones, try keeping a zillion tentacles straight. Jellyfish don't seem to mind when they get a snarl in their "hair." As long as they can glide through the water, they'll keep swimming. If they're not careful, smaller jellies can get caught in a larger jellyfish's tentacles too. In an aquarium, scientists use a glass rod to help untie the knot, if needed.

My, what BIG lips you have!

Well, HELLO, there!

Presenting Mr. Rock and Roll, also known as Cup Coral! Coral are wildly colorful—and wildly misunderstood—creatures. They may look like flowers, but they're really a type of underwater animal that spends its days eating, swaying in the water, and looking pretty. Oh so pretty!

Scientific Name:
   Dendrophyllia gracilis
Size: A single polyp can
   grow up to 12 inches tall
Habitat: Warm waters in the
   Indian and Pacific oceans
Diet: Small bits of meat

This **underwater** rock star gets its **color** from the **algae** that **live** inside it.

The Rainforests of the Sea

Nearly 25 percent of all marine creatures depend on coral to survive. Healthy coral are brightly colored. But when these sensitive creatures don't have everything they need to survive, they turn white. Overfishing, pollution, and invasive species all threaten coral.

Coral Close-ups

Coral come in a bonanza of shapes, sizes, and colors! Many coral are made up of tiny, soft polyps, which are translucent animals like jellyfish. Each polyp has a hard base. When a polyp lands on a rock, it divides and multiplies. Then, thousands of polyps connect to one another to form a colony that acts as one structure. The more structures a colony grows, the more places there are for fish and other sea creatures to live. A colony can live for centuries and join together to form reefs large enough to be seen from outer space.

Psychedelic, Baby!

Sunny-side Up

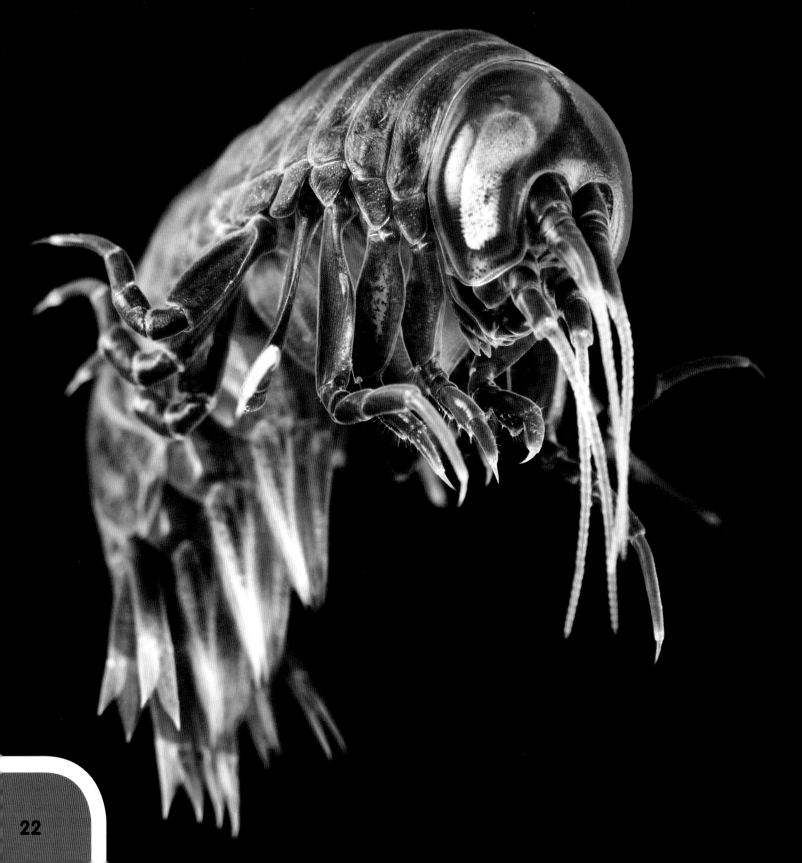

The ocean shall be mine! Muahhahaha!

Creatures great and small make their home in the ocean. This crustacean is about the size of your thumb, but it makes a big impact. Hundreds of marine animals depend on zooplankton for food. These little guys also know how to travel in style. They hitch a ride under the bells of jellyfish and make themselves at home, feasting on jellyfish eggs and whatever the jellyfish eats.

Scientific Name:
Hyperia galba
Size: .5 to 1 inch long
Habitat: Inside jellyfish in North Atlantic and Pacific Oceans
Diet: Jellyfish eggs and the food eaten by jellyfish

Crustaceans are sometimes called "underwater **bugs**" because, like insects, they belong to the **Arthropoda** phylum.

Crusty Creatures
Crustaceans have hard shells and lots of legs. They include everything from crabs to lobsters—and hyperia galbas.

Hide and Seek

Coleman shrimp sightings are rare—maybe because they know just how to blend in. The red-and-white Coleman shrimp lives on the fire urchin, which is known for its toxic touch. But this species has developed the ability to survive the urchin's painful stingers.

Scientific Name:
Periclimenes colemani
Size: Less than an inch long
Habitat: Deep off of the coast of Indonesia
Diet: Algae and plankton

"What is a **scientist** after all? It is a **curious** man **looking** through a keyhole, the keyhole of **nature**, trying to know what's going on."
–Jacques Cousteau

Masters of Disguise
Many animals use camouflage to blend in and hide from predators. Some change their colors or their shape. Others find a safe place to hide or look more intimidating than they actually are.

Somewhere Over the Rainbow

Legs shine bright...
There are so many legs.
Too many to count.
At night.

27

King of the Worms

Meet the creepiest, crawliest critter of the deep: King Ragworm. Like all annelid worms, it has a segmented body, moveable bristles, and a long body cavity. Many, like this one, have a disturbing number of legs. And most can regrow their tails! It may be marine royalty, but the king ragworm spends much of its time burrowed in sand and mud. Don't underestimate it though. When it's time to defend its territory, it won't hesitate to bite or thrash about violently. A nasty fight can end with one or more worms in a knot.

Scientific Name:
Alitta virens
Size: Up to 47 inches long
Habitat: Northern Hemisphere
Diet: Carrion, small fish, crustaceans, and mollusks

This **worm's** "legs" are actually **parapodia**, which act both as **legs** and **gills**.

Sound the Alarm!

When they're competing for resources, king ragworms go to war with each other, but like frenemies, they also depend on each other. They look to each other to detect traces of ragworms that have been eaten or left behind in the water by a predator after an attack. At the first sign of dead ragworms, one ragworm sounds the alarm and the others head for safety.

In a Different Light

To our earthly eyes, this coral is throbbing with color. But it depends how you look at it. Out of water, a coral may look brown and dull, because coral evolved to be seen underwater where light is transmitted differently. That same coral can look stunning underwater, because its fluorescent pigments absorb and reflect different colors.

Scientific Name: Favia
Size: Less than an inch in diameter
Habitat: Atlantic and Pacific Oceans
Diet: Krill, brine shrimp, and plankton

The **knobby ridges** that form the **surface** of this **coral** give it the **nerdy** nickname **Brain Coral**.

Coral Wars

Corals need their space. If there are other corals in the area, watch out! They'll use their tentacles to capture food—and fend off other corals from feeding in the same area.

An Angry Clown

What kind of clown can't turn a smile upside down? A clownfish!
The good news is that with their bright white stripes, clownfish
are as easy to spot as a clown wearing a big red nose.

Scientific Name:
   Amphiprion percula
Size: 2 to 5 inches long
Habitat: Indian and
   Pacific Oceans
Diet: Other small fish

Scientists think the **moonlight** on extra **bright nights** helps **clownfish** know when it's **time** to **mate**.

Queen of the Clowns

Clownfish live in groups, with one female
and up to five males. The female is
always the largest in the group.

Diving Deep

Microscopic photography is revealing thousands of creatures we never knew existed. Diatoms are very simple creatures, but the shapes they take vary nearly as much as snowflakes. Some are round and barely move. Others are long and glide through the water. They're found around the world in mud, water—and the stomachs of the many animals that eat them.

Each **diatom** is **surrounded** by a thin wall of **silica**–the same compound that makes up **glass**.

Scientific Name: Scientists have identified 16,000 different species of diatoms!

Size: Single-celled

Habitat: Pretty much anywhere that's wet

Diet: Most make their own food in the same way plants do

Do You Zig or Zag?

Some diatoms float through the world all alone. But others live in colonies. Together they can form strange ribbon, fan, zigzag, or star shapes.

Glub. Glub. Grub.

A day in the life of a goby fish is filled with swimming and eating. It relies on its wide mouth to eat, build a home, and get where it wants to go. A Hawaiian goby species has even found a way to use its mouth as a suction cup to climb up the 300-foot-tall waterfalls it lives in. Gobies come in a rainbow of colors. They're often found burrowing in sand or mud. They come out to feed, but when it's time to stay home, they use their fins as suctions to grab hold of rocks and stay secure.

Only the Best for My Little Goby

To make sure the world always has more gobies, these fish lay eggs, attach them to a shell or rock, and then the males guard them carefully. Well, kind of. They guard the eggs whenever the female gobies are watching. But otherwise, they're off duty.

Scientific Name: Gobiidae
Size: 2 to 20 inches
Habitat: Throughout the world, most often in the tropics
Diet: Meat eaters, many act as parasites, feeding from the bodies of larger fish

Some **gobies** share **homes** with burrowing **worms**, pea **crabs**, or snapping **shrimp.**

Wild Thing

The ocean lays just beyond our feet, but it might as well lay on another planet. Humans have explored less than 10 percent of it. Like the king ragworm, this is a type of anneid worm, but its colors are positively freaky deaky! And because it was just discovered, scientists don't know much about this polychaete except that it can pull its tentacles inside its body when it needs to hide. The tentacle with the bulb at the end closes the tube so nothing can get inside.

Scientific Name: Unidentified polychaete from the serpulidae family
Size: .5 inch
Habitat: Great Barrier Reef
Diet: Plankton and other tiny underwater creatures

Many **polychaetes** are **named** after **Greek gods** and **goddesses**.

Boldly Going Where No One Has Gone Before

Deep under water, conditions are harsh for sea life—and photographers. It's dark and very cold. Explorers use wet suits to stay warm, make special signals to communicate with each other, and breathe through oxygen tanks. But the glory of seeing something no one has ever seen or getting a shot that reveals the amazing way life survives underwater makes it all worth it.

Up, Up, and Away!

Whichever way the wind blows—or more accurately—whichever way the waves go, this brown-banded beauty goes with the flow. It drifts along with the current and uses its tentacles to scoop up food. Jellies that eat lots of shrimp have a yellow glow to them. Those that eat other crustaceans may look more pink or purple.

Scientific Name:
 Aurelia limbata
Size: Umbrellas grow 24 to 30 inches wide
Habitat: North Atlantic and Arctic Oceans
Diet: Plankton and mollusks

This **ghostly** ice queen **thrives** in very **cold waters**.

Simplicity in Motion

Jellyfish use their mouths in more ways than one. They eat, drink, squirt water, and discard waste from a single opening in their bell.

Underwater Pixies

Itty-bitty, teeny-tiny pygmy seahorses use camouflage to hide from predators. They live on coral sea fans that hide them perfectly. Baby pygmies are born a dull brown color, but they change color to match their home. Pygmies born on orange sea fans become orange. And pygmies born on purple sea fans become purple. They grow bumps to match the texture of the sea fans. Then they hook their tails around a branch and settle in, safe from the ocean's currents.

Scientific Name:
Hippocampus bargibanti
Size: Less than an inch tall
Habitat: Corals in tropical waters
Diet: Small crustaceans

Each **morning**, pygmy seahorses **greet** their **mates** with a special **dance** that includes **rubbing** snouts.

You Are Now Entering The Twilight Zone

Pygmy seahorses live in a mysterious layer of the ocean called "The Twilight Zone." Sunlight rarely reaches this area, and little is known about it.

A Torpedo of Color

There are nearly 300 types of squid in the world. They can change colors depending on whether they are chasing after prey, escaping a predator, attracting a mate, or telling another squid, "I see you." A single squid can flash nearly 35 different color combinations. Many also have ink sacks. When another creature of the deep attacks, they squirt a cloud of ink and make their getaway.

Scientific Name:
Sepioteuthis sepioidea
Size: Up to 8 inches
Habitat: Caribbean reefs and off the coast of Florida
Diet: Small fish, mollusks, crustaceans

Squids **whoosh** through the **water** by **squeezing** water through a **hole** under their **eyes**.

Whatcha Lookin' At?
Caribbean reef squid have a larger eye-to-body ratio than any other animal on Earth. They use their powerful eyes to see in deep, dark waters.

The Labyrinth Awaits

A mysterious light twists and turns. You follow it, spiraling deeper and deeper. Is it a portal to another world? As you look closer, you see it's a shell—just like the kind you find on the beach. It's mysterious, glowing in a way that makes you sure that if you could hold it to your ear at just the right angle, you would hear a song of mystical whale calls—which makes it just like every other shell. Mysterious and ordinary all at once.

Scientific Name: Tonna galea
Size: 6 to 10 inches
Habitat: Caribbean Sea and Indo-Pacific waters
Diet: A wide variety of marine animals, including sea cucumbers

The **sulfuric acid** in its **saliva** helps this **snail kill** its **prey.**

Eye Spy

Next time you're at the beach, bring a pocket microscope with you and look at the sand. You'll find each grain looks like its own strange planet.

47

Spotlight on Seashells

We spend hours at the beach, admiring their beauty, but there's still a lot we don't understand about how marine animals build their shells. What we do know is shells come in all different shapes and sizes. They grow as the creature inside grows. Over time, shells may become cracked or chipped in battle, and their colors may change based on what's in the water. But their main job is to keep clams, snails, and mollusks safe from predators.

Unforgettably Grand

1,000 Shades of White

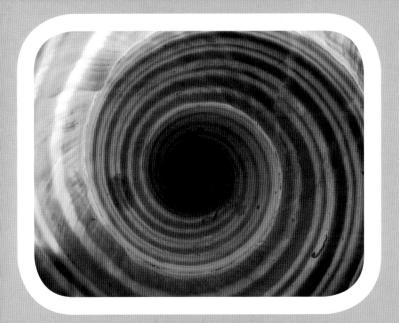

Spiraltastic

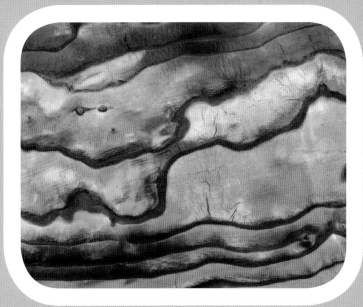

Iridescent Wonder

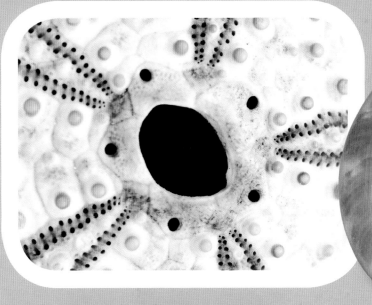

Uniquely Urchin

Rise and Shine, Sleepyhead!

Brush your teeth.
Brush your hair.
(Just don't use
the same brush!)

Shine On!

This pipsqueak punk is as squishy (although maybe not as cuddly) as a teddy bear. This is just one strange version of the many very weird, very strange nudibranches that can be found at the bottom of the sea. There are more than 3,000 types of these sea slugs, and new ones are being found every day.

Scientific Name:
Flabellina verrucosa
Size: .5 to 1.5 inches
Habitat: The White Sea
Diet: Jellyfish and colonies of hydrozoa

Nudibranches use the **tentacles** on their **heads** to **hunt**.

Graceful Gills

The word *nudibranch* means "naked gills." Their feathery spikes act as gills, helping them breathe deep underwater.

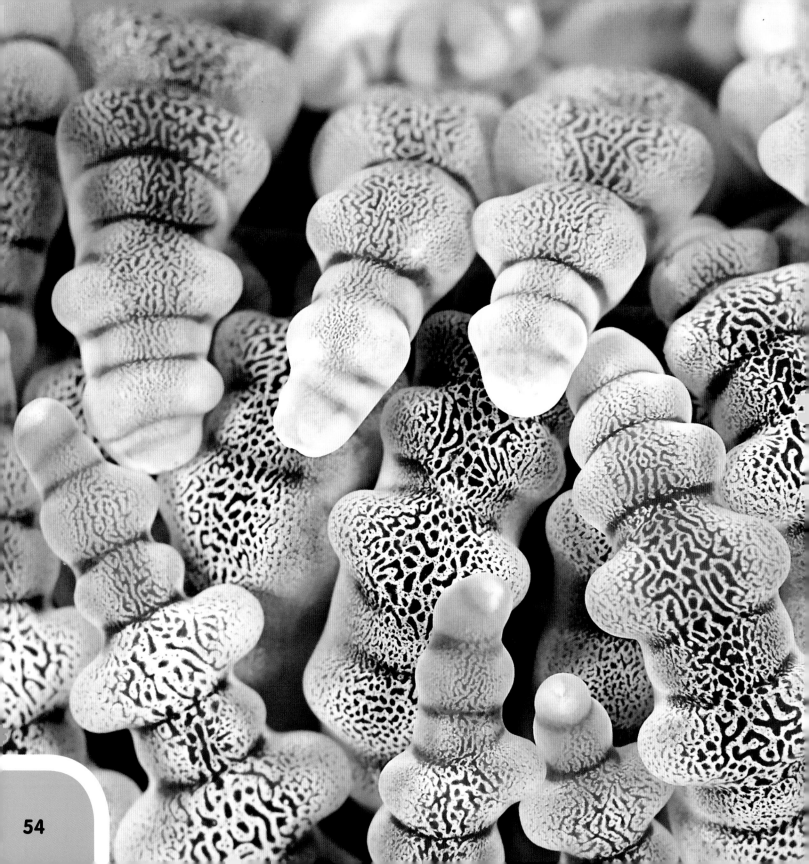

Wiggly, Jiggly, Painful Little Stinkers

Sea anemones are known for their soft tentacles that float in the water like flower petals blowing in the wind. But they aren't as innocent as they look. Their tentacles are filled with venom. As prey passes by—zap! They strike, stinging their next meal until it's paralyzed and can be eaten alive.

Whee!

Most anemones attach themselves to a rock, a shell, or even the back of a crab. And once they find a home, they're unlikely to move, but some have been seen somersaulting across the sand!

Clownfish often make their **homes** in **bended** anemones and are sometimes called "**clown** anemones."

Scientific Name: Heteractis aurora
Size: Tentacles grow up to 2 inches long
Habitat: Tide pools and warmer waters
Diet: Plankton or anything else caught in their stinging tentacles

Parallel Worlds

The creatures found underwater are so strange that the scientists who study them can feel like interstellar travelers, crossing through a wormhole into mysterious new dimensions. Where else would you meet a spotted jellyfish with "oval arms"?

Scientific Name:
Mastigias papua
Size: 4 to 12 inches
Habitat: South Pacific Ocean and coastal waters off Hawaii and Puerto Rico
Diet: Plankton

It's not just **backbones** that jellyfish are missing. They manage to navigate our oceans without **heads, hearts,** or **brains**!

Invertebrates

Invertebrates are animals like jellyfish, worms, and spiders that don't have a backbone or skeleton. Like jellyfish, most invertebrates are symmetrical and move slowly.

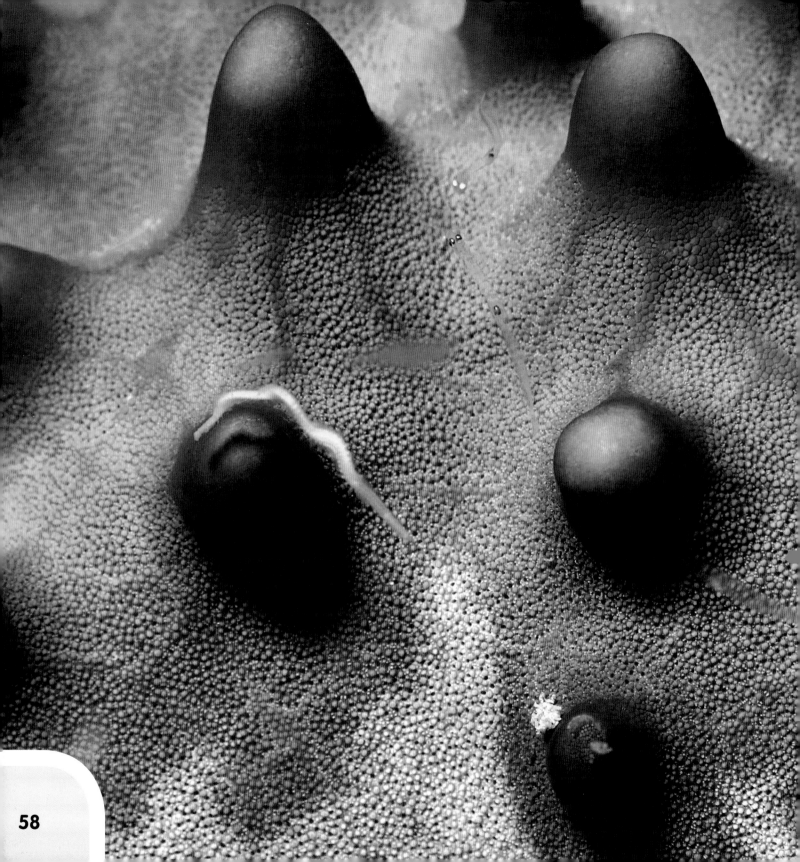

One Tough Cookie

Meet the world's scariest starfish. The knobby sea star. It's covered in black bumps that look like miniature volcanoes. They don't do much except scare away predators. But the adaptation works so well that some small animals stay safe by making their homes on the surface of the knobby starfish. Few predators dare to disturb them there. Would you want to snack on something that looks like it's about to blow up?

Scientific Name:
   Protoreaster nodosus
Size: Up to 12 inches across
Habitat: Tropical waters of
   the Pacific ocean
Diet: Coral, sponges, sea
   snails, urchin

Some people think the **bumps** on this **starfish** look like **horns**. Others say they look like **chocolate** chips. Or the black **stripes** football players **paint** under their eyes! What do you think they look like?

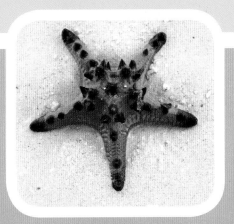

A Five-Star Water System

Starfish are perfectly adapted to life in the water. The water in their bodies gives healthy sea stars their plump shape. They move by taking in water and pumping it to the hundreds of feet that lie beneath their legs. And instead of using blood to move nutrients through their bodies, starfish use water.

Sea Angel

It may look like a butterfly gliding across the night sky, but this sea slug uses its wing-like feet to swim, not fly. And things go from graceful to gross when it uses a glob of mucus to trap plankton. Spiked tentacles are used to capture larger prey, which is then swallowed whole. Clione can survive up to 1,600 feet under water and go longer than a year without eating. They're known as "the potato chip of the sea" because so many sea animals eat them (and can't stop at just one)!

Each **clione** starts **life** as a **male** and becomes a **female** when it's **larger**.

Scientific Name: Clione limacina
Size: About 1 inch long
Habitat: Arctic Ocean and colder parts of the Pacific and Atlantic oceans
Diet: Other limacina

Protecting our Oceans

Every year on June 8th, scientists and ocean lovers celebrate World Oceans Day. There are many non-profit organizations you can get involved with to help protect our deep, blue seas and the amazing creatures that call them home.

Behind the Lens

Now it's your turn! Grab a camera and start shooting whenever you see something that amazes you or makes you curious to learn more. If you want to go macro without spending too much money, snap a macro lens band over a cellphone camera. Whatever camera you use, these tips will help you get started.

The flash lights the subject.

The shutter acts like a camera, opening and closing to let light into the camera for short periods of time.

The lens is the curved piece of glass that light travels through before reaching a sensor or film inside the camera.

A tripod keeps the camera steady.

The size of the opening in the lens is the aperture. It's measured in fractions.

The focal point is the part of the image that's sharp.

The depth of field is the distance between the parts of an object that are in focus. In micro and macro photography, this distance is very small.

Some lenses have a short focal length and produce a wider angle of view. Other lenses have a longer focal length.

Aperture Scale

| f/1.4 | f/2.8 | f/5.6 | f/8 | f/16 | f/22 |

Large aperture ←——————————→ Small aperture
More light strikes image sensor ←——————————→ Less light strikes image sensor
Shallow Depth of Field (Focus) ←——————————→ Deep Depth of Field (Focus)

Index

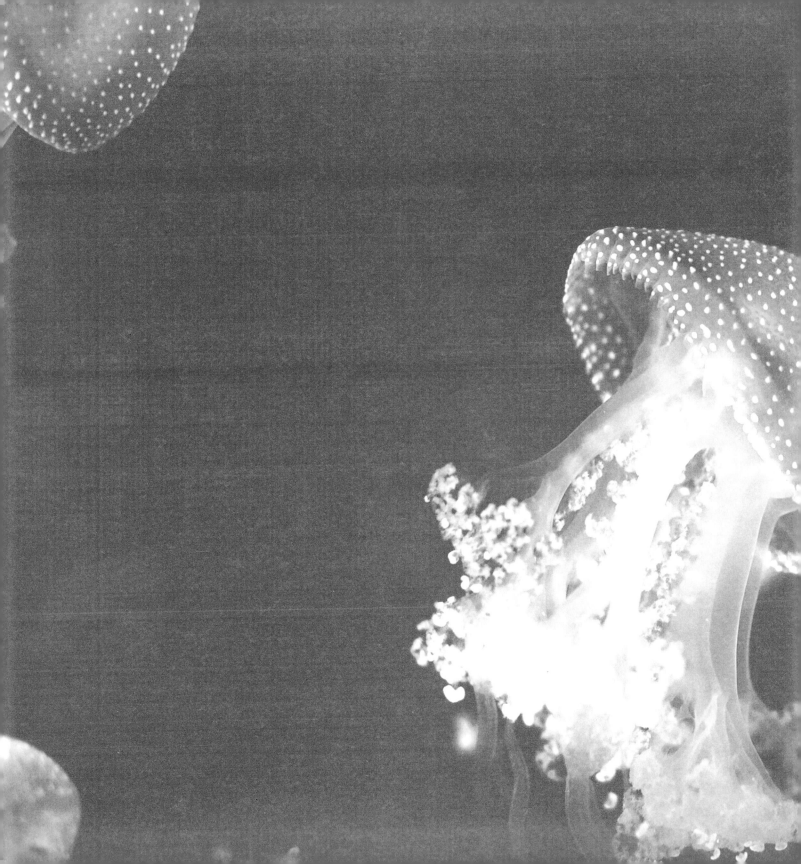